Contents

YOU CHOOSE
BOOKS

OLYMPIANS VS TITANS

AN INTERACTIVE MYTHOLOGICAL ADVENTURE

by Jessica Gunderson

illustrated by Carolyn Arcabascio

Raintree is an imprint of Capstone Global Library Limited, a company incorporated in
England and Wales having its registered office at 264 Banbury Road, Oxford, OX2 7DY
– Registered company number: 6695582

www.raintree.co.uk
myorders@raintree.co.uk

Edited by Mandy Robbins
Designed by Ted Williams
Illustrations by Carolyn Arcabascio; cover illustration by Nadine Takvorian
Picture research by Kelly Garvin
Production by Katy LaVigne
Originated by Capstone Global Library Ltd 2017
Printed and bound in China.

ISBN 978 1 4747 3767 8
21 20 19 18 17
10 9 8 7 6 5 4 3 2 1

British Library Cataloguing in Publication Data
A full catalogue record for this book is available from the British Library.

Acknowledgements

Bridgeman Images/Prometheus and Zeus (Jupiter) battling the Titans (chromolitho),
European School, (19th century) / Private Collection / © Look and Learn, 102
Artistic elements: Shutterstock: Alex Novikov, Eky Studio, reyhan, Samira Dragonfly,
Tymonko Galyna

We would like to thank Dr Laurel Bowman of University of Victoria for her invaluable
help in the preparation of this book.

Every effort has been made to contact copyright holders of material reproduced in this
book. Any omissions will be rectified in subsequent printings if notice is given to the
publisher.

All the Internet addresses (URLs) given in this book were valid at the time of going to
press. However, due to the dynamic nature of the Internet, some addresses may have
changed, or sites may have changed or ceased to exist since publication. While the
author and publisher regret any inconvenience this may cause readers, no responsibility
for any such changes can be accepted by either the author or the publisher.

YOU are a powerful god caught up in a war between two groups of ancient Greek gods. The Titan god Cronus must defend his throne against his children, the Olympian gods, led by the mighty Zeus. The wisdom of the Titan god Prometheus will also play a crucial role. What path will you take to make sure that your side comes out victorious?

Chapter One sets the scene. Then you choose which path to take. Follow the directions at the bottom of each page. The choices you make determine what happens next. After you finish your path, go back and read the others for more adventures.

YOU CHOOSE the path you take through this mythical adventure.

The beginning

According to Greek myth, the universe was once a dark, swirling void called Chaos. Gaia, Goddess of Earth, was born out of the swirls of Chaos. She made the mountains and the sea. She also created the God of the Sky, Uranus.

Gaia and Uranus had 18 children. The first 12 were gods called Titans. The next three were Cyclopes – huge beasts with one eye in the middle of their heads. The last three were monsters called the Hundred-Handed Ones. Each had 50 heads and 100 arms. Gaia loved all her children, but Uranus was terrified of them.

Turn the page.

Uranus imprisoned the Cyclopes and the Hundred-Handed Ones in Tartarus, a dungeon deep within Earth. He was also afraid the Titans would overthrow him, so he pushed them back into Gaia's womb.

Gaia seethed with anger. Her son Cronus vowed to help her. Gaia released Cronus from her womb and gave him a sharp sickle. That night, Cronus crept to his sleeping father and killed him. With Uranus gone, Gaia released the Titans from her womb and the monsters from Tartarus.

But Cronus turned out to be as power-hungry and fearful as his father. He imprisoned the monsters in Tartarus again and sent Campe, a she-dragon, to guard them.

Cronus married another Titan called Rhea. Every time Rhea had a baby, Cronus gulped it down, trapping it in his belly.

When Rhea had her sixth child, Zeus, she sent him to a cave on the island of Crete. Then she wrapped a rock in blankets and gave it to Cronus. He swallowed it whole, thinking it was his child.

On Crete, Zeus became a strong god. He decided to save his siblings and punish his father. When Zeus found Cronus, he mixed a magical herb into a drink. Disguised as a servant, Zeus served Cronus the drink. The drink caused Cronus to vomit, releasing Zeus's brothers and sisters. Cronus suddenly found himself facing his furious children. He knew they meant war.

The gods are going to battle, and you are going with them. What role will you play in this epic war?

To be Cronus, turn to page 11.

To be Zeus, turn to page 43.

To be Prometheus, Titan god of wisdom, turn to page 69.

Chapter 2

Cronus and the Titans

You stare down at your children glaring back at you. Your greatest fear has come true. They stand ready to overthrow you.

Zeus steps forward. "You aren't fit to rule the universe," he says. "Surrender or fight!"

You stand tall, towering over your children and roar, "Fight, of course!"

Your children run to Mount Olympus to prepare for war. You retreat to your palace on Mount Orthrys and call the other Titans. They gather around your marble throne.

Turn the page.

"My children want to overthrow me," you explain. "They are preparing for war."

"We need a plan," your brother Crius says.

You shrug. "What for?" you ask. "We have strength on our side!" You flex your muscles and grin. "We are Titans. They'll never beat us."

"Don't be so sure," your nephew Prometheus warns. "We need a solid plan."

You scratch your head, but thinking has never been your strong suit. "Okay then . . . we'll attack them first," you say finally.

"This won't go well," Prometheus says. He blathers on with some more advice, something about strategy and guarding your door and releasing prisoners. You have trouble following his words, so you stop listening.

Another nephew, Atlas, steps forward. "I'll lead the war," he offers. He looks you up and down. "You're too old to lead anyway."

You bristle. You're not too old! Are you?

To listen to Prometheus's advice, turn to page 14.

To choose Atlas as leader, turn to page 16.

To lead the Titans yourself, turn to page 17.

Sighing, you realize Prometheus knows things you don't. You should probably listen to him.

"Tell me your strategy again," you say.

"First, we need to wait for the Olympians to make their first move," he begins.

"No," you interrupt. "I am strong! I must act!"

Prometheus frowns. "Knowledge is stronger than muscles."

"Impossible," you mutter.

"Second, you should release your siblings from Tartarus," Prometheus continues.

You look around, confused. All of the Titans are right here.

"Not *these* siblings," Prometheus says, irritated. "Your *other* siblings – the Cyclopes and the Hundred-Handed Ones."

You'd forgotten about them.

"They may help us," Prometheus advises. "You don't want Zeus to get to them first."

Your monstrous siblings scare you. A shiver creeps up your spine.

"There must be another way," you argue. You press your fingers to your temples to think.

"I've got it!" you say. "We could ask for help from the river-god Cocytus."

Cocytus is the son of your brother Oceanus. He rules the frozen waters in the Underworld prison of Tartarus. Prometheus shakes his head.

"What is your decision?" Atlas asks.

To release the Hundred-Handed Ones and the Cyclopes, turn to page 18.

To ask Cocytus for help, turn to page 21.

You decide to let Atlas lead the war against the Olympians. He is young and strong, and he seems to have a good head on his shoulders.

"We must meet the Olympians head-on," Atlas says. "We'll win this war in no time."

You nod in agreement. Prometheus shakes his head but doesn't say anything.

Atlas leads the charge to Mount Olympus. You storm the mountain, and the Olympians meet you. Zeus launches an arrow in your direction. It merely bounces off your shoulder.

The Olympians are no match for our brute force, you think.

You stomp your foot, and a nearby mountain crumbles. In answer, the Olympians launch more arrows. The battle has begun!

Go to page 30.

"I'm not too old!" you cry. You flex your muscles and feel your shoulder pop. You wince.

"Are you sure, Uncle?" Atlas chuckles.

"I rule the universe," you cry. "No one rules me. Remember, I defeated Uranus."

"While he was sleeping," Atlas mutters.

"And with help from your mother," Prometheus adds.

You don't care for your nephews' attitudes. But Prometheus has given you an idea. Maybe you should ask your mother, Gaia, for help. On the other hand, you are ready to get this measly war started so you can go back to ruling the universe in peace.

To ask Gaia for help, turn to page 24.

To go straight to war, turn to page 28.

Maybe Prometheus is right. Maybe the Hundred-Handed Ones and the Cyclopes will help you. The more hands, the better, right?

You make your way to the Underworld.

"Hellooo?" you call as you descend into the gloomy pit. Your voice echoes off the fiery walls.

"I would hate to be imprisoned down here," you mumble to yourself.

"Look who has arrived," a voice cackles.

Campe, the she-dragon guard of Tartarus, glides up to you. From the waist up, she is a beautiful woman. But the rest of her body is gruesome. At her waist sprouts the heads of 50 beasts – lions, boars and snakes. The beast heads snarl at you, and you step backwards.

Campe laughs and thumps her scaly dragon-tail. "What can I do for you?" she asks.

You look past Campe at the dungeon. The Hundred-Handed Ones and the Cyclopes bang on the prison bars. One Cyclops stares at you, his one eye circling and glaring.

"Release the monsters," you tell Campe.

"Never!" she hisses. "You told me to guard them to the death. And that is what I'll do."

"I am the god of the universe," you remind her. "You will do as I say."

"Release me instead," Campe says. "I will help you win your war."

"If you release us, we'll fight for you," a Hundred-Handed One calls.

"But only if you promise never to imprison us again," a Cyclops adds.

Turn the page.

You aren't sure whom to trust. Campe has always served you well, but she seems bothered by guard duty. Your monstrous siblings might turn on you too. And you don't want to make promises you can't keep.

To attempt to free the monsters, turn to page 23.

To release Campe from guard duty, turn to page 36.

You venture to the entrance of Tartarus and call out, "Cocytus!"

You hope you don't have to go into the Underworld to find him. Even though you are the god of the universe, Tartarus scares you.

Cocytus rises from the Underworld. He looks cold. Icicles cling to his eyebrows. You explain the situation with the Olympians.

"Can you help?" you ask. "When we win, I'll reward you. Perhaps another frozen lake or two."

"What do you want me to do?" Cocytus asks.

"I'd hoped you might have an idea," you say.

Cocytus shakes his head. "Military strategy isn't my talent. Apparently it's not yours either."

You're insulted, but you need his help.

Turn the page.

"Prometheus says to release the Cyclopes and the Hundred-Handed Ones from Tartarus so Zeus can't use them against me," you say.

"Or I could thaw the waters and flood the Underworld," Cocytus suggests.

"How would that help?" you ask.

"Then Zeus can't get to them," Cocytus explains impatiently.

You agree, and Cocytus disappears into Tartarus. Soon you hear rushing water. *My plan worked!* you think. *I'm as clever as Prometheus!*

When you return to Mount Orthrys, you find that Atlas has rallied the Titans under his command while you were gone. You decide to accept him as military leader. You've done enough thinking for the day anyway.

Go to page 30.

"Step aside," you order Campe.

She doesn't move.

You raise your spear. Your only choice is to slay her. You launch the spear, but she catches it and throws it aside. Then she turns on you.

With one swift flick of her giant, scaly tail, Campe throws you across the universe.
You land in a pit feeling bruised and defeated.

How can I defeat the Olympians if I am so easily beaten by Campe? you wonder.

Your confidence is irreparably shaken. You swallow your pride, give up your fight, and allow the Olympians to take rule of the universe.

THE END

To follow another path, turn to page 13.

To learn more about the war between the gods, turn to page 103.

Your mother helped you defeat your father, so you decide to ask her for help. You find her reclining against a large mountain.

"Goddess of Earth," you say, "the Olympians wish to overthrow me and take over the universe. You helped me defeat Uranus once. Will you help now, too?"

"You have committed no evil deeds?" she asks.

You think long and hard. You can't remember anything evil you've done. And you don't see what that has to do with anything.

"I'm the strongest Titan!" you say. "I deserve to be ruler."

"Take the battle to the sea," Gaia advises. "There, the best ruler will win."

Turn the page.

When you reach the Aegean Sea, you find the Olympians in the water, clashing with the Titans on the coastline. Zeus launches arrows at your brother Iapetus. Iapetus slams his foot into the sand. The whole Earth shakes. You heave a giant breath and unleash it across the sea. Waves throw the Olympians into the air.

You turn to your siblings and raise your arms, in victory. Crius's eyes suddenly widen. He shakes his head and points behind you. You look back just as an enormous wave crashes down on you. You are pulled out to sea, your arms flailing.

As you flounder about in the sea, you look to the shore and see the Olympians using their shields to float on.

The Olympians are clever, you think as another wave pulls you under.

As you surface with a mouthful of water, you hear Gaia's laughter. Too late, you realize she tricked you. She must still be angry with you for imprisoning the Cyclopes and the Hundred-Handed Ones again. You had forgotten about that. Drat your forgetful mind!

The coastline disappears as wave after wave pulls you out to sea. You are too far out to swim back. You paddle around, hoping that one day the Titans will win the war. Maybe they'll even rescue you. But until then, all you have are seabirds to keep you company. And the laughter of Gaia, echoing from the depths of Earth.

THE END

To follow another path, turn to page 13.

To learn more about the war between the gods, turn to page 103.

Mount Olympus looms in front of you. You can see the Olympians preparing for war atop its highest peak, Mytikas.

"Now what?" your brother Iapetus asks.

You have no strategy, only strength. "Let's stomp our feet," you suggest.

You all stomp your giant feet, and Earth quakes. The Olympians desperately sling their wimpy arrows at you. You stomp until mountains crumble and waves crash in the sea.

Suddenly, the earth breaks apart beneath your stomping feet. You fall into a deep crevice. You keep falling and falling until – SMACK! You hit the bottom with a crash.

You cry out for help, but no one comes. For months you are trapped in the crevice. You try to crawl out, but you keep slipping.

Overhead, you can hear the battle raging. No one seems to be winning.

At last, one morning, Atlas peeks over the top of the crevice. "There you are," he says. He reaches down, and pulls you out.

"I'm the leader of the Titan army now," Atlas informs you. "Your strategy didn't work." He gestures to the crevice and the fallen mountains around you. "Obviously," he adds.

Turn to page 30.

With Atlas as leader, the war rages on for 10 years. The universe shakes with the force of battle. No one seems to be winning.

The war moves from land to sea. In one sea battle, your brother Crius calls out to you. You find him in the depths of the ocean, struggling to hold the Olympian goddess Demeter underwater.

"Help me brother!" Crius asks, struggling as Demeter tries to wrench free.

Just then, Atlas bellows at you. He points to Zeus, who is running along the shore. "Catch him!" Atlas orders.

You feel old and tired. Ten years of fighting has worn you out. You might never catch Zeus anyway. And Crius needs your help.

To help Crius with Demeter, go to page 31.

To obey Atlas and chase Zeus, turn to page 33.

You nudge Crius out of your way and hold Demeter underwater. Crius launches a boulder at an oncoming Olympian. It crashes into the sea.

Your muscles are sore. You are worn out from this war. You wish you were in your palace right now. Demeter keeps struggling to break free.

Suddenly a searing light scorches your eyeballs. Hera, Demeter's sister, is holding up a shield. The reflecting sunlight is blinding you. You stagger back, and the goddesses escape.

In the distance you hear a battle and run towards it. As you cross the war-torn land, you see Zeus in the distance. He halts you with an up-stretched hand.

"Surrender, Cronus!" he says.

"Not a chance," you scoff.

Turn the page.

"If you surrender now," he says, "I'll send you to rule over the Isle of the Blessed. If you don't, I'll throw you in Tartarus for eternity when we win this war."

You don't want to give up your rule over the world. And the Isle of the Blessed is so far away. But you are tired of fighting. And you don't want to risk imprisonment in Tartarus.

To accept Zeus's offer, turn to page 38.
To keep fighting, turn to page 40.

You chase Zeus across mountains and valleys, through seas and over islands. Suddenly you realize he is going to Tartarus. You steel your nerves and follow him into the dungeon.

You race forward and find Zeus with his sword raised over Campe, the she-dragon guard of Tartarus. He is about to cut her in half. Then no one will stop him from releasing your monstrous siblings. And they hate you. No doubt they would attack you.

"Stop!" you cry.

Zeus stops mid-swing and stares at you.

"I think we can work this out," you tell him.

"I'm listening," Zeus says.

But you haven't thought this far ahead.

"Umm," you stall.

Turn the page.

"How about this?" Zeus says, clearly annoyed. "You surrender, and I'll send you to rule over the Isle of the Blessed."

You don't want to surrender your position as ruler of the universe. But you're beginning to doubt that the Titans will win this war, especially if the Cyclopes and Hundred-Handed Ones are released and side with the Olympians. Perhaps your strength can get you out of this tight spot.

"But know this," Zeus adds, "if you do not accept my offer, I will throw you in Tartarus once we win this war."

To accept Zeus's offer, turn to page 38.

To fight Zeus, turn to page 39.

You decide to release Campe from guard duty. With her slithering tail and fierce beast-heads, she will certainly scare the Olympians away. And you can live happily as ruler of the universe again.

"You may leave Tartarus and join the Titans," you tell her.

She gives you a wide grin. Her tail slashes through the air and nearly knocks you over.

"I'll never join the Titans!" she cries.

Your eyes widen in fear. "But – " you begin. Before you have a chance to finish your sentence, Campe slaps her scaly tail against you, hard.

You fall to the ground. Campe unlocks the dungeon door and rolls you inside. She slams the door and twists the lock, licking her lips.

A Cyclops looks at you with his one eye. "Now you're one of us," he grunts.

You shiver. Then you become angry. "Release me!" you shout. "You can't keep me down here. I am the god of the universe!"

Campe strokes her beasts. "Not anymore!"

You spend the rest of your days in Tartarus. When the Titans eventually lose the war, Zeus imprisons them in Tartarus too, so at least you have the company of your siblings.

THE END

To follow another path, turn to page 13.

To learn more about the war between the gods, turn to page 103.

You decide being ruler of the Isle of the Blessed is better than risking an eternity in Tartarus. You agree to Zeus's terms.

Zeus unleashes a cry for the war to stop. The sky stops flashing. The seas calm their ferocious waves. All of Greece is silent and at peace.

True to his word, Zeus sends you and your fellow Titans to Isle of the Blessed, a lonely island in a faraway ocean. Ruling the isle is nothing like ruling the universe, but at least you still have some power. You begrudgingly accept your fate and enjoy your reign over the Titans.

THE END

To follow another path, turn to page 13.

To learn more about the war between the gods, turn to page 103.

You lunge at Zeus and tackle him. As the two of you struggle, Campe looks on, mildly amused.

Just as you are getting the upper hand, a Cyclops throws something to Zeus. Sparks fly, and a thunderbolt slams against your chest. You fall backwards.

A thunderbolt? you think. *Where did that come from?*

When you finally sit up, you look around. Tartarus is empty. You decide to go back to Mount Orthrys to gather your thoughts, what few of them you have.

As you emerge from Tartarus, you hear the rumble of battle. You've never been one to avoid a good fight, but your head hurts.

To join the battle, turn to page 40.

To return to Mount Orthrys, turn to page 41.

You choose to fight, but you find the Titans are losing the battle at hand. The Olympians have some new weapons. Poseidon carries a three-pronged trident. When he slams it to the ground, the mountain you are standing on crumbles. Then Zeus zaps you with a thunderbolt until your beard goes up in flames.

"Surrender!" they shout.

Terrified, you cry, "I give up!"

Zeus sends you and the other Titans to the faraway Isle of the Blessed. But he has a special punishment for your nephew Atlas because he led the Titans in battle. He must hold up the heavens for eternity.

THE END

To follow another path, turn to page 13.

To learn more about the war between the gods, turn to page 103.

You are just sitting down on your massive throne when the palace door swings open. The Olympians storm in, with YOUR weapons! Poseidon also carries a trident, made by a Cyclops. You assume that your monstrous siblings have escaped Tartarus and joined the Olympians.

Poseidon bangs the trident on the ground. The whole ground shakes, and you fall off your throne. You are trying to get back up, when ZAP – a thunderbolt hits you.

"I give up!" you cry.

Zeus takes you prisoner. You and the other Titans are doomed to an eternity in Tartarus.

THE END

To follow another path, turn to page 13.

To learn more about the war between the gods, turn to page 103.

CHAPTER 3

Zeus and the Olympians

You and your siblings have suffered too long under Cronus's rule. It's time to take back Greece. First, you need a home base. You settle on Mount Olympus, the tallest mountain in Greece, and you call yourselves the Olympians. You can't conquer Cronus alone, so you ask for your siblings' advice.

"The Titans are gathered on Mount Orthrys," Hades says. "We should attack them there."

"I think we should take the war to the sea," Poseidon counters.

To attack on Mount Orthrys, turn to page 44.

To wage war in the sea, turn to page 45.

You agree to attack the Titans on Mount Orthrys. You don't have many weapons – only bows and arrows. You're hoping to catch the Titans off guard so they surrender quickly.

You, your brother Hades, and your sister Hestia charge Mount Orthrys. Your sisters Hera and Demeter and your brother Poseidon hide at the bottom, ready to help. As you climb the mountain, a Titan steps in your way. You reach for your bow.

"Don't shoot!" he says. "I am Prometheus, Cronus's nephew. Cronus is an unjust ruler, and I intend to help you win this war."

Can you trust him? you think. *Is this is a trap?*

Hades is suspicious too.

"Capture him!" Hades yells.

To capture Prometheus, turn to page 47.

To trust Prometheus, turn to page 51.

"The Titans won't expect us to attack by sea," you say. "We can surprise them."

You and the rest of the Olympians follow the river to the Aegean Sea. Your upbringing on the island of Crete has made you a strong swimmer.

Finally you see Mount Orthrys rising into the sky. The Titans are lounging on the shore, unaware of your approach. On the count of three, you pummel them with arrows.

They don't expect the attack, but they react quickly when they see you and your siblings. The Titans draw their weapons – spears, swords and javelins. They storm into the water with a battle cry. You dodge flying spears and fling more arrows in their direction. The sea churns with the impact of the battle.

Turn the page.

More Titans stream down from Mount Orthrys. The shore is packed with Titan warriors. There's nowhere to escape. Hestia swims up to you, ducking underwater as a javelin shoots towards her.

"We should ditch our shields," she says, panting. "They're just weighing us down. Then we can swim away faster."

She's right. The shields don't offer much protection from the giant Titan weapons, and they're heavy. Without them, you could make a quick escape. But you're not sure you want to give up fighting quite yet.

To ditch the shields, turn to page 48.

To keep the shields and fight on, turn to page 50.

"I will never trust a Titan," you say.

Hades tackles Prometheus. You drag him to Mount Olympus, where Hestia guards him.

The Titans soon storm Mount Olympus. Your army launches every arrow you have but you eventually surrender to the Titans. Cronus hurls you as hard as he can into the Underworld prison of Tartarus. Prometheus lands next to you.

"You are prisoner too?" you gasp.

Prometheus nods. "For betraying the Titans and trying to help you," he explains.

You are defeated. You should've listened to Prometheus, after all.

THE END

To follow another path, turn to page 13.

To learn more about the war between the gods, turn to page 103.

You command the Olympians to drop their shields and fall back. Without the shields, you are light and fast. You swim quickly out to sea. Up ahead you see a familiar island. It's Crete, your childhood home. Once on shore, the Cretans greet you with happiness.

"Stay," they plead. "We'll keep you safe here."

Just then, another voice breaks in. It comes from the sky and from the land. It is your grandmother, Gaia.

"You cannot stay here. You must defeat Cronus," she calls. "Can I count on you, Zeus?"

To stay on Crete, turn to page 60.

To listen to Gaia, turn to page 61.

You decide to keep your shields. Cronus is on shore with the other Titans. He heaves a giant breath. The sea rises into a huge wave that is heading straight towards you.

"Quick!" Hera cries. "Put our shields together to make a raft."

You latch your shields together and climb on. The wave whips you high into the air, but the raft stays steady. After the wave passes, you see an eagle circling overhead. You are about to call to the eagle when you hear a cry from the shore. It's a Titan called Prometheus. You aim your bow and arrow at him, but he holds up his hands.

"Let me help you defeat Cronus," he says.

Should you trust a Titan? It could be a trick.

To accept Prometheus's help, go to page 51.

To call to the eagle, turn to page 63.

The Titans outnumber you. You need all the help you can get.

"What help can you offer us?" you ask Prometheus, lowering your bow and arrow.

"My knowledge," he says. "I have foresight. I can see things that will happen in the future."

"So what should we do next?" you ask.

"Go to Tartarus and release the Cyclopes and the Hundred-Handed Ones," he says.

You have heard of the Hundred-Handed Ones and Cyclopes. The monsters have been imprisoned in the Underworld dungeon since Cronus came to power. They just might help you defeat the Titans.

You make your way to Tartarus, deep underground. Tongues of fire curl at your feet.

Turn the page.

You are nearing the dungeon of Tartarus, when an enormous roar rattles your bones. You crouch behind a boulder and peer around it.

A terrifying creature paces back and forth in front of the dungeon. She has a woman's head but the body of a dragon. Dozens of beast heads circle her waist like a belt. You shudder. She must be the famed she-dragon, Campe.

You gaze behind her at the dungeon, where the Hundred-Handed Ones and Cyclopes beat against the dungeon's bars.

You might be small enough to slip through the bars and convince the monsters to help you. You aren't sure you are strong enough to slay Campe anyway.

To sneak into Tartarus, go to page 53.

To fight Campe, turn to page 54.

You sneak into Tartarus to ask the Cyclopes and Hundred-Handed Ones to help you fight Cronus. But first you must get past Campe.

Campe paces in front of the dungeon. As you creep from your hiding place, her tail swings and hits you. In a flash, Campe throws you into the air. You soar through the crevices and flames of Tartarus and land with a giant splash in a swirling river. The river goddess Styx rises from the waters and stares down at you.

"Zeus," she says. "I've been waiting for you."

Before she can explain, strong talons grip your shoulders and lift you into the air. You look into the face of a great eagle. He seems to be carrying you out of Tartarus, but to where you don't know.

To let the eagle carry you away, turn to page 63.

To wrestle away from the eagle and listen to Styx, turn to page 64.

You draw your sickle, grab a small rock and step from the shadows. You hurl the rock as far as you can. Campe lumbers towards the sound. You leap onto her tail, and bury the sickle into her neck. You cling to her tail as she whirls around to face you. She hisses. Her breath steams in your face. But her wound is deep. She heaves one last breath and slumps to the ground. You hop off her tail and pry the dungeon key from her grasp. Then you turn to the prisoners.

"I will release you from Tartarus," you say. "But you must help me win the war against Cronus and the Titans."

"We can make special weapons for your army," a Cyclops says.

"And we have hundreds of arms to hurl stones," a Hundred-Handed One adds.

Turn the page.

You release the monsters. Once above ground, the Cyclopes make special weapons for you and your brothers. When they are finished, a Cyclops called Arges hands Poseidon a three-pointed spear called a trident.

"Strike the trident against the ground, and Earth will shake and the seas will churn," Arges says.

He hands Hades a metal helmet. "This helmet will make you invisible."

Lastly, Arges hands you a metal thunderbolt.

"With this thunderbolt, you can make lightning strike, anytime and anywhere," he says.

Hades slips on the helmet and disappears.

"Now that I'm invisible," his voice says, "I can sneak into the Titans' camp and steal their weapons from under their noses."

You keep staring at your thunderbolt. You can't wait to strike down Cronus and the Titans. With your lightning power, you don't even need the other Olympians. You could take them on yourself.

To attack the Titans yourself, turn to page 58.

To attack the Titans with your army, turn to page 65.

Alone, you make your way to Mount Orthrys. You boldly open the door to Cronus's palace.

Cronus is sitting on his throne, surrounded by the Titans holding their weapons. You launch a thunderbolt at Cronus. A fierce streak of lightning blazes through the air and zaps Cronus with a sizzle.

"Ahh!" he cries.

You are impressed by the force of the lightning bolt.

"The Titans are no match for me," you think, raising another thunderbolt.

Just then, a Titan hurls a spear in your direction. The spear clangs against the thunderbolt, and it clatters to the ground. You lunge for it, but another Titan hurtles towards you and knocks you to the ground.

You reach for the thunderbolt as a spear stabs your hand. You are pinned and can't move. You should have let Hades steal the Titans' weapons. Why did you want all the glory for yourself?

Cronus steps towards you. His robes are singed, but otherwise he's unharmed. He picks up the metal thunderbolt. "Hmm," he says. "With this weapon, I could burn you and the Olympians down."

Knowing you are doomed, you shake your head. "We surrender," you say.

Cronus imprisons you and the other Olympians in Tartarus. You can hear his loud cackle as he resumes his evil rule over the world.

THE END

To follow another path, turn to page 13.

To learn more about the war between the gods, turn to page 103.

You say to your siblings. "We are safe here. Let us rest and then launch a surprise attack."

"No," Poseidon says. "We must defeat Cronus now before he does more damage to the world."

"We will stay here and rest," you say firmly.

That night, the Cretans treat you to a feast. But in the morning, the Olympians are gone.

"They left to fight Cronus," your friends say.

You can't believe they disobeyed your orders. They've even taken your bow and arrow. From afar, you watch battles rage over Greece. When at last the Olympians win, they don't come to get you. You stay on Crete forever, a forgotten god.

THE END

To follow another path, turn to page 13.

To learn more about the war between the gods, turn to page 103.

You don't want to give up your quest to overthrow Cronus, so you decide to listen to Gaia's advice.

"I want you to release my children, the Hundred-Handed Ones and the Cyclopes, from their prison in Tartarus," she tells you. "They will help you defeat the Titans."

You build a raft, and you and the Olympians sail back to Greece under the darkness of night.

"I will go to Tartarus alone," you tell your siblings. You descend into the Underworld, armed with a scythe the Cretans gave you.

In the dungeon, you find Campe, the she-dragon guard, asleep. She wakes from her slumber when you enter. Campe blinks her heavy eyelids at you and rises to her haunches. You didn't imagine she would be so large.

Turn the page.

You lunge forward and bury the scythe in her neck. As she howls in pain, you grab the key from her fingers and open the dungeon door.

The Hundred-Handed Ones and the Cyclopes are grateful to you for releasing them. "We will make you magical weapons to defeat Cronus," a Cyclops called Arges tells you.

For Hades, the Cyclopes make a helmet of invisibility. For Poseidon, they forge a three-pronged trident that will shake the earth and seas. The Cyclopes give you a metal thunderbolt that unleashes lightning.

Go to page 65.

You realize the eagle is an omen of victory. He vows to help you win the war.

In the following battles, the eagle soars ahead to scout out danger. In one battle, it even catches lightning in its mouth and drops it on the Titans. The Titans retreat to Mount Orthrys.

Eventually, you release the Cyclopes and Hundred-Handed Ones from Tartarus. The Cyclopes make a thunderbolt for you, a trident for Poseidon and a helmet of invisibility for Hades. The weapons help you win the war. When the war is over, you send the eagle to the heavens to become a constellation. Every night, you look up and thank him for his help.

THE END

To follow another path, turn to page 13.

To learn more about the war between the gods, turn to page 103.

You pry the eagle's talons from your shoulders and drop into the river. The goddess Styx stands over you majestically.

"My children and I will come to your aid," she says. "But you must promise me the power of death when you win the war. Any god who doesn't swear oaths by me will become mortal."

You agree. You desperately need the help of Styx's winged offspring, the gods Kratos and Zelus and the goddesses Nike and Bia.

The children of Styx fight by your side. When you finally overthrow Cronus, you bestow great honours upon Kratos, Zelus, Nike and Bia. The winged gods never leave your side.

THE END

To follow another path, turn to page 13.

To learn more about the war between the gods, turn to page 103.

Armed with your new weapons, Hades and Poseidon journey with you to Mount Orthrys. The Hundred-Handed Ones follow, ready to pelt rocks at the Titans when the battle begins.

Outside the cave that leads to Cronus's palace, Hades slips on his helmet of invisibility and disappears. You can hear the soft fall of his footsteps as he enters the cave. As you wait, worry sets in. What if his helmet falls off and he is discovered? Your mind swirls thinking of all the ways your plan could go awry.

Just then, a pile of weapons suddenly appears at your feet. Then Hades materializes, helmet in hand, grinning. Excited, you gather the weapons and throw them to the Hundred-Handed Ones. You and your army are now ready to storm the palace.

Turn the page.

As you enter, Cronus stands up, surprised and frantic. The other Titans look around for their missing weapons, confused. Poseidon slams his trident down. The mountain trembles, and Cronus topples to the ground.

Now it is your turn. You raise your thunderbolt. Lightning sears through the palace. Cronus thrashes about on the ground, sparks sizzling on his flesh. He looks up at you, frightened, as you raise the thunderbolt again.

"I give up!" he wails. "You have won the war. Rule over Earth is yours. Just don't strike me with that searing weapon again!"

You lower the thunderbolt. "Throw all the Titans into Tartarus!" you command the Hundred-Handed Ones.

When you emerge from the palace, the sun is shining. The heavens and Earth seem to be smiling down at you. You are now the king of the gods. The world is yours forever.

THE END

To follow another path, turn to page 13.

To learn more about the war between the gods, turn to page 103.

Chapter 4

Prometheus

You watch on as Cronus and Zeus face each other. You have a gift to see the future. You know that an epic war is about to begin. Even your name, Prometheus, means "foresight". You are the wisest of the Titans. Your knowledge would be helpful to each side's cause.

Cronus has not been a fair ruler. He has imprisoned his own siblings, the Cyclopes and the Hundred-Handed Ones, in Tartarus for eternity. He is greedy and loves power more than anything. You are concerned that the world will continue to be a place fraught with battles and war if he remains ruler.

Turn the page.

Zeus seems honest and fair. But he has lived his life on the island of Crete with little knowledge of the outside world. He still has a lot to learn.

"You aren't fit to rule!" Zeus tells Cronus.

"You are just a child," Cronus says to Zeus.

"Prepare for war!" Zeus cries.

Cronus storms up to his palace on Mount Orthrys. Zeus and his siblings make camp on Mount Olympus. You are faced with a decision.

You have the foresight to know that Zeus would make a good ruler in time. But the Titans are your family. Can you turn your back on them?

To side with the Titans, go to page 71.

To side with the Olympians, turn to page 82.

You know some of what is to come, so you can help the Titans make the right decisions in the war. But you're taking a big risk. If the Titans lose the war due to your advice, Cronus won't hesitate to send you to the Tartarus dungeon.

You reach Cronus's palace and approach him.

"Uncle, we need to make a plan," you tell him.

"We don't need a plan. We have strength," Cronus says.

"And even the best-laid plans often go awry," your father, Iapetus, adds.

"Strength won't win this time," you say. "I've had visions that this war will last a very long time and wreak havoc on the universe. The Tartarus prisoners, the Cyclopes and the Hundred-Handed Ones may be the key to winning the war."

Turn the page.

"Hmph!" Cronus shrugs. "I don't believe in your visions."

You draw a deep breath and stand your ground. "Even so, Uncle, we need to have strategies in place to defeat the Olympians."

Cronus waves a finger at you. "I've heard enough, Prometheus. We'll just attack and stomp them out."

The other Titans are murmuring behind you. You can tell they think you need a plan too. You could hold a war council without Cronus. But if you do, you are at risk of angering him. He could send you to Tartarus for defying him.

To hold a war council yourself,
go to page 73.

To accept Cronus's idea of attacking with strength,
turn to page 75.

You bow to Cronus. "Yes, Uncle," you say.

On your way out the door, you whisper to your brother Atlas, "Let's have a war council at the bottom of Mount Orthrys. Spread the word."

He nods, and you step quickly out the door.

You gather the other Titans at the bottom of the mountain, out of Cronus's earshot. "My foresight tells me that we need to release the Hundred-Handed Ones and Cyclopes from Tartarus," you say. "Otherwise the Olympians will use them to their advantage."

The Titans mutter amongst themselves.

"None of us want to go to Tartarus," Atlas finally says.

You strap on your armour. "Then I will go to release them," you say.

Turn the page.

As you are making your way to Tartarus, you hear a great shout. Ahead, you see Cronus waving for your attention. His leg is stuck in a giant crevice, and the Olympians are bombarding him with arrows from their perch on a nearby hill.

"Pull me out, Prometheus!" Cronus cries.

To ignore Cronus and continue to Tartarus, turn to page 77.

To help Cronus, turn to page 79.

You have a bad feeling, but you don't want to argue with Cronus and bear his wrath. Maybe you will have another chance to use what you know about the war.

Cronus appoints your brother Atlas to command the Titan army. Under his leadership, you and the Titans storm Mount Olympus. Your thunderous footsteps shake Earth.

The Olympians are ready for you, though, with arrows drawn. The Titans outnumber the Olympians, but the Olympian gods don't give up. The war rages for several years.

One day, in the heat of a vicious battle, you see a figure coming towards you. As the smoke clears, you see it is a Cyclops. You don't know how he managed to escape Tartarus.

Turn the page.

The Cyclops blinks his eye as he lumbers towards you. You reach for your spear.

"Stop," the Cyclops snarls in a raspy voice. "Cronus finally listened to your advice and released me. I am on your side. I can give you a weapon more powerful than a spear."

You know the Cyclopes are very good weapon-builders. But you aren't sure why Cronus would have released the Cyclops without telling you. The Cyclops takes another step towards you. You know you need to act.

To accept the weapon the Cyclops made,
turn to page 95.

To battle the Cyclops and send him back to Tartarus,
turn to page 101.

You don't have time to spare. You must release the Tartarus prisoners before the Olympians do.

You descend into Tartarus. It is dark, even though flames leap along the path. You find the dungeon where the prisoners are bound in chains.

The dungeon guard, Campe, is a she-dragon. She turns as you approach. The heads of beasts dance around her waist. Campe wags her scaly tail and growls, "What do you want?"

You look at the prisoners. The Cyclopes stare at you with one rolling eye in the middle of their heads. The Hundred-Handed Ones reach for you with their many hands. They are even more grotesque than you remembered.

"I have come to release the prisoners," you tell Campe. "They will help us fight the Olympians."

Turn the page.

"Whatever you say," Campe laughs. She turns the key in the lock, and the prisoners break free.

"Join the Titans to defeat the Olympians," you say. "When we win, Cronus will honour you."

"Never!" a Cyclops called Arges shouts as a Hundred-Handed One puts you in the dungeon.

"We will be joining the Olympians now," Arges says. The monsters turn and run.

"You fool!" Campe laughs. "You thought they would join Cronus? He imprisoned them."

You slump to the ground. You thought you were wise and knowledgeable. But you are now destined to an eternity in the Tartarus dungeon.

THE END

To follow another path, turn to page 13.

To learn more about the war between the gods, turn to page 103.

You dodge flying arrows as you run to Cronus's side. You grasp his arms and tug, and his leg comes loose. But as he tumbles to the ground, the crevice opens wider, and you slide in. You call for Cronus, but he is already bounding away.

With each crash of Cronus's footsteps, boulders roll into the crevice. You duck and cover your head. Suddenly you look up to see Olympians slinging arrows at you.

You look around at the boulders piled at your feet. You could fight back and hurl the boulders at the Olympians. Or, you could call for a cease-fire and tell them what you know about the future of the war. You aren't sure you want to re-join Cronus, anyway, after he just abandoned you here.

To fight against the Olympians, turn to page 80.

To reach out to the Olympians, turn to page 98.

You pick up a boulder and heave it at the Olympians. It hits Zeus, and he falls backwards. You hurl another and another, knocking the Olympians down. Finally, they run away. You pile the remaining boulders on top of each other to form steps and climb out.

When you return to Mount Orthrys, you go straight to Cronus's palace. He is dozing on his throne, snores rattling from his open mouth.

"Cronus!" you shout.

He wakes with a start.

"Your plan to attack the Olympians failed," you tell him. "You ended up stuck in a crevice."

"Yes, but somebody pulled me out."

"That was me," you sigh. "And you just left me there. Are you ready to listen to my plan now?"

At Cronus's nod, you explain to him that the Olympians will use the Hundred-Handed Ones and Cyclopes to defeat him.

"Then we must guard them!" Cronus cries.

"They are already guarded," you say. "We should release them – "

Cronus cuts you off. "I know the perfect guard!" he says, looking straight at you.

He sends you to Tartarus to help Campe, the she-dragon, guard the dungeon. You have no choice but to obey Cronus. You wish your foresight had warned you that you'd spend eternity in the Underworld with an irritable she-dragon before you offered to help your uncle.

THE END

To follow another path, turn to page 13.

To learn more about the war between the gods, turn to page 103.

All signs point to the Olympians winning the war and eventually overthrowing Cronus. You want to help them in any way you can. You know the Olympians will bring stability to the universe.

In the dead of night, you sneak away from Mount Orthrys. By the time you reach Mount Olympus, dawn is breaking. The Olympians are already awake, huddled in a grove of trees. They are making plans to defeat the Titans. You crouch behind a tree and listen.

"By land or by sea?" Zeus is saying.

"By sea!" you say, stepping forward.

The Olympians jump to their feet and reach for their bows and arrows. You raise your right hand to stop them.

"I have come to help you," you say.

Turn the page.

You introduce yourself and tell them of your gift of foresight.

"And you think we should attack the Titans by sea?" Zeus asks.

You nod.

"I agree," says Poseidon.

But Zeus is thoughtful. "We don't have a ship," he says. "I propose an attack by land."

To join Poseidon at sea, go to page 85.

To join Zeus in the land attack, turn to page 86.

You wade out to sea with Poseidon on your shoulders. But you haven't foreseen a good plan of attack. You hope an idea will come to you soon.

Suddenly a roar erupts behind you. You turn to see a huge sea monster emerging from the water. He has gleaming teeth and pointed scales. You hope he's friendly as he surges towards you.

As the monster opens its mouth to speak, you hear singing in the distance. Sweet songs float towards you. The songs remind you of your mother, Clymene, who is an Oceanid sea goddess. She has thousands of sisters, and you wonder if the songs are your aunts calling to you. You could swim towards them and ignore the sea monster, or you could wait and hear what he has to say.

To listen to the sea monster, turn to page 88.

To swim towards the singing, turn to page 90.

You decide to join Zeus in a land attack. You don't want to contradict his leadership.

You and the Olympians rush Mount Orthrys, armed with bows and arrows. The Titans fight back. Flaming spears soar through the air. The whole world shakes with the sounds of war.

After years of fighting, neither side appears to be winning. In the quiet after one particularly brutal battle, you have a vision that Cronus's prisoners – the Hundred-Handed Ones and the Cyclopes – will turn the tide of war. You need to convince Zeus to release them.

As you are on your way to Mount Olympus to tell Zeus of your vision, you hear someone shouting over the next hill. You creep close to investigate and find that it is your brother Atlas, swirling in a river of fire. Smoke billows from his burning limbs.

Atlas sees you and calls out. "Brother! Help me!"

He is a Titan, and you have sided with the Olympians. You aren't sure if you should help him. Helping Atlas would betray the Olympians. But he is your brother. Can you just leave him there to suffer?

To help Atlas, turn to page 92.

To continue on to find Zeus, turn to page 98.

You beckon to the sea monster. He shimmers and transforms into a god. "I am Proteus, a shape-shifting god," he tells you. "Like you, I too can see the future."

Proteus points towards the shore.

"Cronus is about to unleash a great breath and shake the seas," he says. "You should swim to shore immediately."

Proteus shimmers and disappears again.

"Wait!" you say. "What else can you tell us about the war?"

Proteus fades away until only his voice is left.

"Convince Zeus to release the Cyclopes and the Hundred-Handed Ones from Tartarus!" he says.

And then he is gone.

You and Poseidon paddle frantically to shore. You reach land just as you hear Cronus's breath whistling through the air. Waves leap high into the heavens. You have made it just in time. Now you must find Zeus.

On your way to find Zeus, you look up at a distant hill and see a great army approaching under the blazing sunlight. You blink, and the army disappears. It is only a mirage, but the vision gives you an idea. You could mould an army of humans from clay, and breathe life into them. The army could help Zeus defeat the Titans.

To create an army from clay, turn to page 93.

To continue on and find Zeus, turn to page 98.

You tell Poseidon that you will be back and swim towards the singing voices. The voices are hauntingly beautiful. You find yourself mesmerized by them.

You reach a small, rocky island. Lovely women lounge on the island's cliffs. Sweet songs rise from their mouths.

You suddenly realize that they are not your Oceanid aunts. Instead, they are sirens, lovely but dangerous creatures who lure sailors to their deaths with their melodies.

You try to swim away, but the songs have gripped you. You spend eternity entranced by the sirens, unable to escape.

THE END

To follow another path, turn to page 13.

To learn more about the war between the gods, turn to page 103.

Atlas is your brother. You must help him.

Suddenly, lightning knocks you off your feet. You look up to see Zeus, holding a gleaming thunderbolt. You've never seen such a weapon. Then you see the Hundred-Handed Ones and Cyclopes behind him. You realize he's let the prisoners out of Tartarus, and the Cyclopes have made him a powerful weapon of a thunderbolt.

"Traitor!" Zeus yells at you. "Capture him!"

The Hundred-Handed Ones grab you and throw you into Tartarus. When the Olympians win the war, they send the other Titans there too. Their company is slim comfort, as they also view you as a traitor.

THE END

To follow another path, turn to page 13.

To learn more about the war between the gods, turn to page 103.

You instruct Poseidon to find Zeus and tell him to release the monsters from Tartarus. Then you find a cave with soft clay soil to start building your army. You mould the clay into humans and breathe life into them. You then steal fire from the heavens and give it to the humans. They need it for warmth and cooking or they'll die, after all. Zeus will understand once you explain it to him.

You and your human army march to find Zeus, hoping he'll be pleased with your effort. But you have taken so long to create the humans that Zeus and the Olympians have already won the war. And Zeus is anything but pleased by the humans you have created. Nor is he happy that you have given them fire.

"You have stolen fire from the gods!" he thunders. "For this deed you must be punished."

Turn the page.

Zeus chains you to a rock in the Caucasus Mountains. Every day, an eagle pecks at your liver. Because you are immortal, your liver regenerates every night, only to be eaten again and again by the eagle. You hope that someday a strong god will break your chains and rescue you, but until then, you must suffer.

THE END

To follow another path, turn to page 13.

To learn more about the war between the gods, turn to page 103.

"What can you offer?" you ask the Cyclops.

The Cyclops holds out a metal object shaped like a lightning bolt. "Use with care," he says. "This weapon contains the power of the heavens."

You close your eyes for a moment. You have a vision of the lightning and thunder booming from the end of your weapon. You smile. You now have the most powerful weapon in the universe!

You are ready to face Zeus head-on and win the war for the Titans. You will be revered by all Titans forever. Cronus will reward you with a palace and riches. You march excitedly towards Mount Olympus, where the Olympians have retreated, lost in your dreams about your bright future. You are so thrilled with the power of the thunderbolt that you don't realize you have become just as greedy as Cronus.

Turn the page.

In the distance, you see the six Olympians marching down the path leading from Mount Olympus. They look ready for battle.

Your instinct is to hide, but then you remember your thunderbolt. As they near, you step out in front of them.

"Surrender, Zeus!" you cry. You point the thunderbolt at him, waiting for the searing lightning. Nothing happens.

You look up to see Zeus holding something in his hand. It's a thunderbolt, identical to yours.

"What in the – " you start to exclaim. But before you can finish, a bolt of lightning sears into your chest. You fly into the air, with your hair and toga on fire. Your useless thunderbolt clatters to the ground. The Cyclops tricked you!

Zeus's lightning sizzles you again in mid-air. You fall to the ground, and when you sit up, the Olympians are gone. All that's left is the smell of something burning. You realize it's your flesh.

You don't need a vision to know that the Olympians are about to win the war. And you're on the losing side.

THE END

To follow another path, turn to page 13.

To learn more about the war between the gods, turn to page 103.

"I know something that may help you," you tell Zeus. "My visions tell me that if you release the Hundred-Handed Ones and the Cyclopes from Tartarus, they will help you defeat Cronus."

Zeus and the other Olympians talk amongst themselves, until finally Zeus says, "I will go to Tartarus and release the prisoners." He looks at Hera and Demeter. "Guard him while I'm away."

You wait on Mount Olympus under the watch of the two goddesses. You hope your premonition was right. If not, the Olympians might imprison you.

At last, Zeus returns with the Cyclopes and Hundred-Handed Ones. The Cyclopes have made weapons for the Olympians – a thunderbolt for Zeus, a helmet of invisibility for Hades and a three-pronged trident for Poseidon.

Turn the page.

Hades puts on the helmet of invisibility and disappears. He then goes to Mount Orthrys to steal the Titans' weapons. As more battles rage on, Poseidon strikes his trident to the ground, and it knocks the Titans to their knees. Meanwhile, Zeus zaps Cronus with his thunderbolt until he surrenders.

The war is over, and, as you predicted, the Olympians have won. Zeus is now the ruler of the gods. He approaches you gratefully.

"Prometheus, I am in great debt to you," Zeus says. "I would like you to be my top adviser."

You accept Zeus's offer. From then on, you help Zeus rule the gods fairly and honourably.

THE END

To follow another path, turn to page 13.

To learn more about the war between the gods, turn to page 103.

You don't believe the Cyclops. You raise your spear and lunge at him. Just then, an invisible force tackles you and holds you down. You look up to see the Olympian Hades holding you down with one foot, a helmet in his hands.

"A helmet of invisibility!" you gasp. "Genius!"

You want to ask the Cyclops how he made the weapon, but suddenly Poseidon appears, bearing a three-pointed trident. He slams it against the ground. The entire universe shakes, sending you into the air. You soar higher and higher, until Earth is a tiny blue dot and stars twinkle around you. You'll never make it back to Earth. With any luck, you'll become a constellation.

THE END

To follow another path, turn to page 13.

To learn more about the war between the gods, turn to page 103.

CHAPTER 5

King of gods

According to Greek myth, the war between the Titans and the Olympians lasted 10 years. Ultimately, Prometheus sided with the Olympians, though he himself was a Titan. His wisdom and foresight helped him see that the Olympians would be the more just rulers of the universe and would be most likely to win the war. He also knew that the monsters in Tartarus would be key to winning the war.

On Prometheus's advice, Zeus released the Cyclopes and the Hundred-Handed Ones from Tartarus. With the weapons the Cyclopes forged, the Olympians at last won the war.

Turn the page.

Zeus cast Cronus and the Titans into the Underworld prison of Tartarus. For Atlas, the Titans' military leader, Zeus reserved a special punishment. Atlas was boastful of his strength and power. Zeus tasked him with holding the sky on his shoulders for all eternity.

The Olympians wanted to rule fairly. The three brothers, Zeus, Poseidon and Hades, divided rule equally among themselves. Zeus became god of the sky, Poseidon god of the seas and Hades god of the Underworld. Hera became goddess of marriage and family. Hestia was goddess of the hearth and home. And Demeter was goddess of the harvest. Although they ruled equally, Zeus was the leader and called the "king of gods". He tried to rule fairly and balance his own interests with those of the other gods and goddesses.

Zeus appointed Prometheus as his top adviser. Prometheus later formed mortals from clay and offered them the gift of fire. Prometheus's actions angered Zeus because he believed fire should be reserved for the gods. Zeus chained Prometheus to a rock and ordered an eagle to peck out Prometheus's liver. Zeus's son Hercules eventually saved Prometheus from this torture.

Zeus was the father of many other great Greek gods and goddesses, such as Athena, Apollo and Ares. He also fathered children with mortal women. They included Hercules and Helen of Troy. It was said the Olympians maintained their rule from a palace on Mount Olympus, where snow and rain never fell, and the wind never blew.

Turn the page.

Like all Greek myths, the story of the war between the gods helped ancient Greeks make sense of the world around them. In a time before there was much technology or scientific understanding, these stories explained why the world worked as it did.

The myths also showcased the values of ancient Greek society. Justice and wisdom were rewarded, while greed and ignorance were punished. The Greek gods and goddesses were not all-knowing or all-powerful, either. Their human attributes reflected the imperfections of all mankind.

GREEK GODS AND GODDESSES

Atlas Titan god who led the Titans in their battle against the Olympians. Zeus punished him by forcing him to hold the heavens on his shoulders for all eternity.

Cronus Titan god of time and the universe. He let fear and insecurity overtake him, which led him to act selfishly and ultimately be overthrown by his own children.

Hades god of the Underworld and brother to Zeus. His weapon is a helmet of invisibility.

Hera goddess of marriage and family. She is married to Zeus and is often called the queen of the gods.

Poseidon god of the sea and Zeus's brother. Poseidon was strong-willed and had a bad temper. The raging waters of the sea suited his personality. His weapon was a trident.

Prometheus Titan god of wisdom and foresight. The help he offered to the Olympians was critical to them defeating the Titans.

Zeus god of the sky and ruler of the Greek gods. He was known for trying to be just and fair. His weapon was a thunderbolt.

OTHER PATHS TO EXPLORE

1. Gaia had sided with Zeus against the Titans, but after the war, she turned on him. She was upset that Zeus imprisoned the Titans in Tartarus and wanted all gods to live in peace. She enlisted a race of giants to battle the Olympians and overthrow Zeus. A 10-year war between the Olympians and the giants broke out. Do you think Gaia had a right to be angry with Zeus? Whose side would you fight on – Zeus and the Olympians, or Gaia and the giants? Why?

2. Prometheus is credited with creating humans. But Zeus became angry that humans ignored the gods and cared only for their own interests, so he took fire away from them. This meant humans could not cook or keep warm. Prometheus felt sorry for them, so he stole fire back and gave it to the humans. As punishment, Zeus chained him to a rock and instructed an eagle to peck out his liver daily. But Prometheus continued helping the humans. From the rock, he taught humankind how to build houses, sail ships and practice medicine. Why do you think Prometheus continued to help humans?

3. Zeus and Hera married, but before Hera, Zeus had another wife called Metis. When Zeus found out that if Metis had a child, it would overthrow him, he swallowed her whole, not realizing she was already pregnant. Inside Zeus's body, Metis began making a robe and helmet for her daughter, giving Zeus such terrible headaches that he asked another god to split open his head. When his skull split, out jumped his daughter Athena. She became Zeus's favourite child and the goddess of war. Why do you think Zeus felt so threatened that he swallowed his wife? How do his actions compare to his father Cronus's actions?

FIND OUT MORE

Gods and Goddesses of Ancient Greece (Ancient Greece), Danielle Smith-Llera (Raintree 2015)

Greek Myths and Legends (All About Myths), Jilly Hunt (Raintree, 2014)

Tales of the Greek Heroes (Puffin Classics), Roger Lancelyn Green (Puffin Classics, 2009)

WEBSITES

www.bbc.co.uk/schools/primaryhistory/ancient_greeks/gods_and_heroes/
Learn about Greek gods with these fun activities and articles.

www.primaryhomeworkhelp.co.uk/greece/myths.htm
Read about the heroes, monsters and gods of Greek mythology.

GLOSSARY

constellation group of stars that forms a shape

eternity time without beginning or end

foresight act or ability to see into the future

javelin light spear

mortal unable to live forever

Oceanid female sea goddesses

scythe tool that has a curved blade with a long curved handle

sickle tool with a sharp curved blade shaped like the letter "C," and a short handle

talon long, sharp claw

trident spear with three tips; the weapon of Poseidon

womb organ inside a woman in which a baby grows

BIBLIOGRAPHY

Allan, Tony and Sara Maitland. *Titans and Olympians: Greek & Roman Myth*. Time-Life Books. London, UK: Duncan Baird Publishers, 1997.

Apollodorus. *The Library of Greek Mythology*. Oxford, UK: Oxford University Press, 1997.

Barnett, Mary. *Gods and Myths of Ancient Greece*. New York: Modern Publishing Regency House, 1997.

Buxton, Richard. *The Complete World of Greek Mythology*. London: Thames & Hudson, Ltd., 2004. *Gods and Goddesses of Greece and Rome*. Tarrytown, NY: Marshall Cavendish Reference, 2012.

Hesiod. *The Theogony*. Project Gutenberg. http://www.gutenberg.org/files/348/348-h/348-h.htm#link2H_4_0023

Ovid. *Metamorphoses*. Theoi Classical E-Texts Library. http://www.theoi.com/Text/OvidMetamorphoses1.html

Stapleton, Michael. *The Illustrated Dictionary of Greek and Roman Mythology*. New York: Peter Bedrick Books, 1986.

Waterfield, Robin. The *Greek Myths: Stories of the Greek Gods and Heroes Vividly Retold*. New York: Metro Books, 2011.

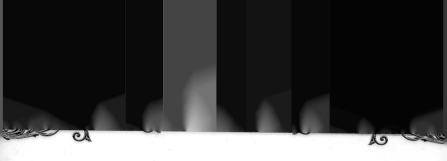